BURIAL OR CREMATION FOR CHRISTIANS?

'Devout men buried Stephen
and made great lamentation over him'
(Acts 8:2)

BURIAL OR CREMATION FOR CHRISTIANS?

A BIBLICAL PATTERN FOR FUNERALS

Adrian V W Freer

wcp

Welford Court Press

Burial or Cremations for Christians? A Biblical Pattern for Funerals

Originally published by EP Books, Faverdale North, Darlington DL3 0PH, England, 2014

Revised and expanded second edition
Published in 2023 by:
Welford Court Press
4 Whitebeam Road
Oadby
Leicester LE2 4EA
United Kingdom
www.webdatauk.wixsite.com/welford-court-press

ISBN: 978-0-9520304-9-2

British Library Cataloguing-in-Publication Data
A catalogue record for this book is available from the British Library.

Printed and distributed by Amazon

DEDICATION

To those Christians who seek to do the Lord's will in both life and death.

ACKNOWLEDGEMENTS

All Scripture quotations are from The Holy Bible, English Standard Version® (ESV®), copyright © 2001 by Crossway, a publishing ministry of Good News Publishers. Used by permission. All rights reserved. Quotations from Holy Scripture are shown in '*italics*'.

The extract of the Apostles' Creed is taken from *The Book of Common Prayer*, the rights of which are vested in the Crown, and reproduced by permission of the Crown's Patentee, Cambridge University Press.

Unless credited otherwise, illustrations are created by the author, reproduced from publications that are out of copyright, images released into the public domain or else permission has been granted by the copyright holder.

Finally, I would like to record my sincere thanks to my wife, Louise, for her encouragement with my literary efforts, her painstaking help with my research, for making many valuable suggestions and for reading the numerous proofs and re-proofs.

Notes to the text are to be found following chapter 8.

CONTENTS

ILLUSTRATIONS

PREFACE

There appears to be a dearth of clear biblical teaching at the present time on the subject of whether Christians should be buried or cremated. Whether this is because death and its surrounding issues are off-limit subjects, or to avoid unsettling those who have already made (unalterable) choices about the burial or cremation of their loved ones, is unclear. Nevertheless the fact remains that when decisions have to be made, many folk are unsure of what is right. Hurried decisions are not always the same as those that would have been made if the matter had been considered under less stressful circumstances.

That being the case, it seemed prudent to address the issue by examining what the Bible has to say, in order that funerals are conducted in the most scriptural manner. Let it be said at the outset that, as a result of my studies, I have become convinced that burial is the correct option for believers.

The standpoint from which this work has been written is that the Bible is God's inspired Word; it is infallible and without error in its entirety; and its commands need to be obeyed, its good examples followed and its bad ones shunned. The relevant Bible references have been quoted throughout and it is strongly recommended that they are referred to in order to gain the fullest historical and cultural understanding.

In this short volume the author has endeavoured to be as balanced as possible, although it is difficult to be impartial when one holds firm convictions on any subject. It is hoped that it will help those who wish to have a clearer understanding of the issues; crystalize the thoughts of those who have already chosen burial but not fully thought through their reasons why; and prompt those who have not considered the subject previously to give the matter the thought it warrants.

By setting out the issues systematically, it is the author's sincere desire that this short volume will be of help to those engaged in pastoral ministry; firstly to assist them as they seek to gain a better understanding of the topic, and secondly in order that they can address the matter logically when they are called upon to offer advice on the burial/cremation issue.

It is also hoped that it will be of assistance when the question arises of how we ought to respond when relatives are considering whether to have a loved one or close friend cremated, and we are called upon to reason the facts sympathetically with them.

As with all things in the Christian life, the submissions offered here should be considered prayerfully and Scripture, taken in context, should *always* be the final arbiter.

Adrian V W Freer
Leicester

Chapter 1

THE BODY AND SOUL AND THEIR ETERNAL DESTINATION

B elievers who have come to a saving faith in Jesus Christ as a result of God's sovereign, elective grace have the assurance of the Bible's promise that, once they die, their immortal soul is at once translated to heaven to be forever with their Lord and Saviour. There is no warrant anywhere in Scripture for erroneous views such as soul-sleep, annihilation, purgatory or penance (see 2 Corinthians 5:8).

Whilst the fact that our immortal soul is at once received into glory is a great comfort at a time of bereavement, there does come the point when a decision has to be made about what to do with our earthly body. Should it be buried or cremated — and does it really matter anyway?

As we shall see, there are many pointers to the fact that burial should be the favoured option among Christians; although it should be stated that the Bible does not give any absolute *command* in the matter. Nevertheless, as we shall discover later, some of the patriarchs did give very precise instructions that they were to be buried.

Let it be made clear at the outset that, although neither of the practices is in itself *sinful*, that does not negate the fact that careful and sympathetic thought should be given to decide how and where our loved ones' final remains should be laid to rest.

THE SERIOUS ISSUES OF LIFE AND DEATH

More than anyone else, Christians do consider carefully the serious issues of life and death. The whole focus of the gospel is bound up with our eventual and final destination after death — whether we end up in heaven or hell! That being so, it is surely wise for believers to do a little practical preparation for their demise beforehand. Unless our Lord returns in the meantime, it is an undisputable fact that we shall all die at some point.

Bereavement is always a traumatic time for those left behind, and Christians are *not* immune to that grief and sorrow. After all, death is a constant reminder of the outworking of sin in the world. It is only right that we mourn and lament over the loss of a loved one, but we do not grieve in the same way as unbelievers who have no hope whatsoever (see 1 Thessalonians 4:13-14). We have on record that our Lord was moved to weep at the grave of his friend Lazarus (John 11:35).

THE WISDOM OF PLANNING AHEAD

To alleviate the anguish for our families as much as possible, a little forward planning can spare those left behind some of the stress. The provision of a funeral plan, prior purchase of a burial plot, choice of venue and minister for the thanksgiving service, and the selection of hymns and readings are all things that can be done in advance. As time progresses there is no reason why amendments cannot be made as circumstances change.

By making arrangements beforehand, the deceased has the comfort of knowing that things will proceed in accordance with their wishes and that decisions do not have to be made at the last moment. That must surely ease the burden in some measure.

Tranquillity of an English churchyard

A funeral plan purchased in advance enables many practical choices to be made and once death occurs, a telephone call is all that is required to set things in motion.

If time is taken to select a burial plot it can be in the graveyard of choice and located in a position that is appropriate; if desired, adjacent to loved ones. By so doing it is likely that, when the time comes for the plot to be used, most of the surrounding plots will have been utilized and the area will have matured and mellowed. It is comforting to know in advance precisely where one's final resting place will be.

Making arrangements for the funeral service is not a morbid affair, but rather making our wishes known in order that the service will be conducted in accordance with the deceased's requests.

In the passage referred to later on concerning Joseph, it will be noted that he gave strict instructions about what was to happen to his remains after his death. That must surely be a prudent example to follow.

Once decisions have been made and set down on paper, they can be signed and sealed in an envelope and passed on to one or more trusted relatives or friends for safe keeping until our demise.[1] Lodging instructions solely in our will may not necessarily be the wisest move as it may not be consulted until after the funeral has taken place. Probably the best course of action is to record our instructions both separately with relatives or friends, *and* in our will, to be absolutely sure.

Including a list of the significant events, dates and places in one's life will considerably assist whoever is left with the task of composing the eulogy. It is sometimes amazing how little succeeding generations know about the early life of the deceased.

MADE IN THE IMAGE OF GOD

In the account of creation we are told that man is a special creation and totally unlike any other animals or creatures. Man was specifically created in the image of God (see Genesis

1:27) and therefore, if we are made in his image, we surely cannot treat that image, once life has departed from it, like a mere piece of garbage and dispose of it irreverently; but rather we should give it respect.

Scripture teaches us that the bodies of believers are temples of the Holy Spirit, and as such they need to be treated with dignity. We do not belong to ourselves anymore because we have been purchased at great cost by God who has redeemed us. In 1 Corinthians 6:19-20 we are reminded: *'Or do you not know that your body is a temple of the Holy Spirit within you, whom you have from God? You are not your own, for you were bought with a price. So glorify God in your body.'* To treat such a temple to burning to cinders is disrespectful to something set apart as holy by the precious blood of Christ.

BURIAL OR CREMATION?

To aid us in our study, it is appropriate to look at examples from Scripture to guide us when we come to decide whether we should be buried or cremated. There are numerous precedents and these all confirm that burial has always been the preferred method of laying the corpse to rest for God's people from the very earliest times.

It is pertinent to note that nowhere in the Bible is there any example of the body of a believer being burned. There is the account of disobedient King Saul whose disfigured body was burned after his death at the hands of the Philistines; but even then his remains were eventually given a proper burial once his bones had been recovered (see 1 Samuel 31:8-13; and 2 Samuel 21:12-14).

Many of the biblical terms that are used for death such as *'... slept with his fathers'* (this phrase is actually used on thirty-six occasions in Scripture; for example, King Ahaz in 2 Kings 16:20); *'he died and was buried in the tombs of his fathers'* (King Josiah in 2 Chronicles 35:24); and *'fallen asleep'* (New Testament believers who have died but have seen the risen Christ, in 1 Corinthians 15:6), all imply that the body of the deceased is left to lie in peace and slowly return to dust, rather than being rapidly consumed by fire.

The Mount of Olives and Jerusalem

When King Hezekiah was laid to rest in the same tombs as King David, in Jerusalem, his ancestor had already been resting there for almost three hundred years. We read in 2 Chronicles 32:33: *'And Hezekiah slept with his fathers, and they buried him in the upper part of the tombs of the sons of David, and all Judah and the inhabitants of Jerusalem did him honour at his death. And Manasseh his son reigned in his place.'*

At the time when Simon Peter delivered his sermon at Pentecost he referred to the fact that King David's tomb was still there: *"'Brothers, I may say to you with confidence about the patriarch David that he both died and was buried, and his tomb is with us to this day'"* (Acts 2:29). When Peter was speaking, David had already been buried for over one thousand years. In some way even the commonplace acrostic 'RIP', Rest in Peace, just does not seem to fit in with cremation. It is nigh impossible to correlate 'resting in peace' with the mental image which is visualized when a body is consigned to the flames of a crematorium furnace.

BODIES HAVE TO BE TREATED WITH DIGNITY

There is something inherently grounded into the human conscience that demands that bodies are recovered and treated with dignity, sometimes at a great deal of cost and effort. That is the reason why relatives take the trouble to ensure that bodies are recovered from accident sites, or repatriated from foreign countries, and laid to rest among familiar surroundings.

When people go missing, long searches are made for them, extending long after there is any chance of them being found alive, and that is not just because we want to know what happened to them, it is also in order that a funeral can take place.

Once bodies have been buried they are invariably left to lie undisturbed over the centuries and it is only in very extreme situations that they are ever moved. If circumstances dictate that this has to happen, then great care and sensitivity are always exerted over their removal and preservation.

During the construction of Rutland Water, St Matthew's Church at Normanton (built in 1764) would have been submerged as the church is located forty yards within the perimeter and below the level of the reservoir. It was therefore deconsecrated in 1970 and the coffins interred in the church were removed from the vaults and reburied, either at Edith Weston or Edenham. Since then the floor of the church has been raised above the water line and an embankment and causeway constructed. Today, with its distinctive tower designed by Robert Cundy, Normanton Church remains a memorial to the county's historic and aristocratic past and is the most notable landmark in the area.

Normanton Church, Rutland Water

Chapter 2

ACCOUNTS OF BURIAL IN THE OLD TESTAMENT

I n our deliberations on how to dispose of our mortal remains reverently, we cannot do better than to look at the examples, and there are many, that we are given in Holy Scripture in both the Old and the New Testament.

EXAMPLES OF BURIAL IN THE OLD TESTAMENT

In the earliest book of Scripture written, Job clearly foresaw that he would be buried when he declared his faith in his God and predicted his eventual resurrection, in Job 19:25-26: '"*For I know that my Redeemer lives, and at the last he will stand upon the earth. And after my skin has been thus destroyed, yet in my flesh I shall see God.*"'

After the Fall, when death first entered the world, God told Adam that he came from dust (see Genesis 2:7) and that he would eventually return to dust; and this statement most surely implies a slow decay (after burial) rather than a swift burning by fire. Genesis 3:19 records God's words: '"*By the sweat of your face you shall eat bread, till you return to the ground, for out of it you were taken; for you are dust, and to dust you shall return.*"'

When Abraham's wife Sarah died, he bought the cave of Machpelah together with the field in which it stood, which was to the east of Mamre, in order to bury her. He purchased the land from Ephron the Hittite for four hundred shekels of silver. One whole chapter, Genesis 23, is devoted to the transaction and if such a large portion of Scripture is devoted to the purchase of a burial plot, it must surely be significant. It is relevant to note that Abraham insisted on buying the land rather than accepting it as a free gift as Ephron had originally offered. Notice also that Abraham wanted the transaction to be done legally and openly.

Mamre (Hebron): the site of the cave of Machpelah where Abraham buried his wife Sarah

When Abraham himself died, his two sons, Isaac and Ishmael, buried him in the same grave as Sarah (Genesis 25:7-10); and in turn when Isaac died his two sons, Esau and Jacob, buried him in the same place as Abraham (Genesis 35:29 and Genesis 49:31). It was the same grave in which Rebekah and Leah were also interred (see again Genesis 49:31) although Rachel was buried at Bethlehem (Genesis 35:19). We see here the establishment of the pattern of

22

gathering the bodies of the deceased together into one place. This will be discussed further in chapter 4.

Genesis 49:28-33 gives the account of the death of Jacob and we learn the very precise instructions that Jacob gave to

Bethlehem

his sons that he was to be buried. In verses 29-30 we read: *'Then he commanded them and said to them, "I am to be gathered to my people; bury me with my fathers in the cave that is in the field of Ephron the Hittite, in the cave that is in the field at Machpelah, to the east of Mamre, in the land of Canaan, which Abraham bought with the field from Ephron the Hittite to possess as a burying place."'* The following chapter (Genesis 50:1-14) gives the account of Joseph travelling to Canaan and burying Jacob there in accordance with his father's wishes.

Although Joseph was one of the most powerful men in Egypt, and could have had a lavish state funeral there if he

Burial of the Judges of Israel		
JUDGE	BURIED	BIBLE REFERENCE
Othniel	Not stated	~
Ehud	Not stated	~
Shamgar	Not stated	~
Deborah & Barak	Not stated	~
Gideon	Buried	Judges 8:32
Abimelech	Not stated	~
Tola	Buried	Judges 10:2
Jair	Buried	Judges 10:5
Jepthah	Buried	Judges 12:7
Ibzan	Buried	Judges 12:10
Elon	Buried	Judges 12:12
Abdon	Buried	Judges 12:15
Samson	Buried	Judges 16:31

Even at a time of waywardness and apostasy for the nation, many of the Judges of Israel were buried, as the table indicates had so wished, the Bible records that he gave instructions before his death (in Genesis 50:24-26) that his bones should be carried up from Egypt to the promised land. We are told in the passage that he was embalmed and put into a coffin. Later on, it is recorded that the Children of Israel had brought Joseph's bones up from Egypt at the exodus (Exodus 13:19) to bury them at Shechem, in a piece of land that Jacob had bought from the sons of Hamor (Joshua 24:32).

ISRAEL IN THE TIME OF THE JUDGES

In the time of the Judges, the destitute Naomi decided to return to Bethlehem from Moab, and her daughter-in-law Ruth the Moabitess resolved to forsake her people in order to accompany Naomi. As they departed, Ruth affirmed her trust in the only true God in what is probably the most moving declaration of faith in the whole of Scripture, *"'Do not urge me to leave you or to return from following you. For where you go I will go, and where you lodge I will lodge. Your people shall be my people, and your God my God. Where you die I will die, **and there will I be buried**. May the Lord do so to me and more also if anything but death parts me from you'"* (Ruth 1:16-17, emphasis added).

One of the consequences of becoming a part of God's people was that Ruth would adopt the Jewish custom of burial. Even though the time of the Judges was a period of great apostasy, the Jews still kept up the practice of burial. The above, and the table, already show quite a substantial list of people from early history who were buried, but the Bible records many other individuals from the period who were similarly laid to rest: Deborah, Rebekah's nurse (see Genesis

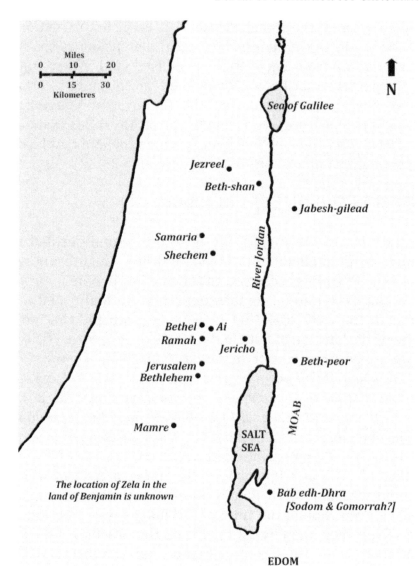

Notable locations in the land of Canaan in Old Testament times

35:8); Aaron (Deuteronomy 10:6); Miriam, Moses' sister (Numbers 20:1); Eleazar, Aaron's son (Joshua 24:33); and likewise Joshua (Joshua 24:29-30).

Furthermore there were those whom the Lord struck down in the wilderness because they had grumbled against God and craved for meat. All of these disobedient people were buried as Scripture testifies: *'Therefore the name of that place was called Kibroth-hattaavah, because there they* **buried** *the people who had the craving'* (Numbers 11:34, emphasis added). The footnote informs us that the name of the location where this event took place means 'graves of craving'.

When King David died we are told that he was buried, in the city of David (1 Kings 2:10).

In the accounts of the lives and deaths of the kings of Judah and Israel recorded throughout Kings and Chronicles, it documents over and over again that when they died they were *buried* — the kings of Judah in the city of David and many of the kings of Israel in Samaria: Solomon in 1 Kings 11:43; Rehoboam in 1 Kings 14:31; Abijam in 1 Kings 15:8; Asa in 1 Kings 15:24; Jehoash in 2 Kings 14:16; Hezekiah in 2 Chronicles 32:33; and so on.

With regard to the prophets, we read that after Samuel died he was buried: *'Now Samuel died. And all Israel assembled and mourned for him, and they buried him in his house at Ramah'* (1 Samuel 25:1). In 2 Kings 13:20 it records that when Elisha died, he too was buried, *'Then Elisha died, and they buried him.'*

Although kings were normally buried inside cities, the common people were customarily buried outside the city walls. This is implied in 2 Kings 23:6 when speaking of

Josiah's reforms: *'And he brought out the Asherah from the house of the Lord,* **outside Jerusalem, to the brook Kidron,** *and burned it at the brook Kidron and beat it to dust and cast the dust of it* **upon the graves of the common people***'* (emphases added).

GOD *BURIED* MOSES

Finally in our study in the Old Testament, we have to note that when Moses died we are informed that God buried him. It records in Deuteronomy 34:5-6: *'So Moses the servant of the Lord died there in the land of Moab, according to the word of the Lord, and he buried him in the valley in the land of Moab opposite Beth-peor; but no one knows the place of his burial to this day.'* It has to be remarked that if God chose this manner of laying to rest the body of his servant, it gives us a clear example to follow.

One would have thought that if God did not want Moses' tomb to be found he would have burnt his remains beyond recognition, but nevertheless he chose burial. Despite all the archaeological excavations that have taken place in the Holy Land over the years, the site has never been located.

Chapter 3

ACCOUNTS OF BURIAL IN THE NEW TESTAMENT

Before we proceed and look at examples of burial in the New Testament, it is appropriate to mention that the apostle John records that, in our Lord's time, burial was the normal and accepted practice of the day. Referring to the burial of Jesus, in John 19:40, he says, *'So they took the body of Jesus and bound it in linen cloths with the spices, **as is the burial custom of the Jews'*** (emphasis added).

Burial places for ordinary people were generally situated in solitary and unfrequented places: on the sides of

The Garden Tomb, Jerusalem

mountains, in gardens (hence the Garden Tomb), in fields, adjacent to houses, or by the roadside. Tombs which were located alongside the road would be whitened once a year to identify them and warn travellers in order that they might not mistakenly touch them and become defiled, hence the 'whitewashed tombs' of Matthew 23:27.

THE DEMON-POSSESSED MAN

In the New Testament account of Jesus healing the demon-possessed man at Gadara, in Mark 5:1-20, we are told that he lived among the tombs, which were away from the city. No doubt this solitary and gloomy location meant that he would be left undisturbed for much of the time. After the demons had entered the pigs and drowned, the herdsman fled and

Gadara

told the account of what had occurred: *'The herdsmen fled and told it in the city and in the country. And people came to see what it was that had happened'* (v. 14).

When John the Baptist was beheaded by evil King Herod, at the request of Herodias' daughter, we read that John's disciples took his body and buried it (Matthew 14:12).

BURIAL OF THE LORD JESUS

The most notable example of burial in Scripture, of course, is the interment of our Lord Jesus after his sacrificial death on the cross for his people, and the Bible records many very precise details.

Even before he was born, the Old Testament prophets testified to the fact that Jesus was to be buried. Writing over one thousand years prior to Jesus' death, inspired by the Holy Spirit, King David made this Messianic prophesy in Psalm 16:10: *'For you will not abandon my soul to Sheol, or let your holy one see corruption.'* The prophet Isaiah testified to the same fact three hundred years later: *'And they made his grave with the wicked and with a rich man in his death, although he had done no violence, and there was no deceit in his mouth'* (Isaiah 53:9).

Before considering the matter of Jesus' death and burial it is necessary to go right back to his birth and observe that when the wise men came from the east to worship Jesus, they presented him with very significant gifts. Gold was to signify his kingship, frankincense his high priestly office, and myrrh to indicate that he would die (see Matthew 2:1-12).

Myrrh emanates from a white resinous gum that exudes from the bark of a tree which resembles an acacia, and it hardens on contact with the air. It was customarily employed to anoint the body of the deceased (amongst other purposes), as we shall shortly see. The prophetic gift of myrrh, significantly given by Gentiles, confirmed that even at his nativity Jesus was destined to die and be *buried*.

One speculates whether, when the women prepared the

Myrrh

spices to anoint Jesus' dead body, Mary would have brought the container of myrrh which she had kept all through the years and it was now coming into the use for which it had originally been intended. Being the devout woman that she was, that would be highly likely.

After Jesus' crucifixion we are told that Joseph of Arimathea went to Pilate and asked for his body in order that it might be decently buried (John 19:38). Nicodemus brought a mixture of around seventy-five pounds[2] of myrrh and aloes to anoint it (John 19:39). These spices were customarily smeared between the layers of clean linen cloth with which the body was wrapped to counteract the odour which would emanate as a result of the putrefaction as the body decayed.

Once Joseph and Nicodemus had prepared the corpse it was then laid in the new tomb which Joseph had previously prepared for his own use by cutting it from the rock

(Matthew 27:60). It was a new tomb and was situated in a garden *'close at hand'* (John 19:42). Notice that Joseph had prudently made prior preparations for his own demise. Subsequently a stone was rolled over the entrance to secure it. Such was the trouble these two disciples took, and respect that they had for Jesus and his lifeless body. The Jews did not embalm bodies as was the Egyptian practice.

Aloes

After the burial of Jesus we are told that the women prepared spices and ointments on the evening of the crucifixion (Luke 23:56) and then, when the Sabbath had ended, they returned to the tomb to anoint, as they supposed, Jesus' dead body (Luke 24:1). Once again it was their intention that the body, although lifeless, was to be treated with the utmost propriety and dignity.

Aliens living in Israel were also granted the rite of burial and the chief priests and elders used the thirty pieces of silver which Judas Iscariot had received for betraying Jesus, and later returned, to buy the potter's field as a *burial* place for strangers (Matthew 27:7). The site probably contained numerous excavations where clay had been removed in order to make pottery and these would in turn be used as burial plots.

ACCOUNTS OF BURIAL RECORDED IN ACTS

Scripture records that Stephen, the first martyr to die after the early church was formed, and who was stoned at the instigation of the Jewish religious leaders, was laid to rest by being buried. Acts 8:2 records that, *'Devout men buried Stephen and made great lamentation over him.'* The action of these 'devout men' was to bury rather than cremate his body.

In another episode in the life of the early church, Ananias and Sapphira were both struck dead as a result of their hypocrisy in lying to the Holy Spirit, and we are informed that they were both separately carried out by the young men to be *buried* (see Acts 5:1-11).

It is relevant to underline the fact that these last two incidents took place shortly after the outpouring of the Holy Spirit at Pentecost, when the New Testament church was in the process of being formed. At that time the apostles and church were being guided in a very special and direct manner

The stoning of Stephen by Domenico del Barbieri (c.1506-c.1570)

by the Holy Spirit in the way it should function and how believers should conduct themselves.

Chapter 4

THE HOW AND WHERE OF BURIAL

Having looked at the accounts of burial in the Bible it is now appropriate to consider the manner and location in which burial should take place, and once again there are numerous examples to be found in Scripture.

HOW OUR MORTAL REMAINS ARE LAID TO REST

Just as the Jews had a reverence and respect for mortal remains, so should we. Not only was the body buried, it was also carefully prepared and anointed prior to its final laying to rest, as we have already seen.

When our Lord was anointed at Bethany by Mary (John 12:1-8) she took a very expensive ointment made from pure nard[3] (an essential oil extracted from a plant of the Valerian family that grows in India), which cost the equivalent of a year's wages for an agricultural labourer. Mary was commended for this act of devotion which Jesus

Spikenard

described in Matthew 26:12 as a preparation for his burial. Notice that Jesus fully expected that he would be buried. Funerals at the time were often lavish and expensive affairs and this symbolism of our Lord's death and burial signified far more than Mary realized at the time. The perfume was of such a potency that the aroma filled the whole house (John 12:3).

Bethany

When Lazarus was brought forth from the tomb, at our Lord's command, his body was bound with linen strips and his face was wrapped with a separate cloth (John 11:44). Jesus instructed those around Lazarus to, "'*Unbind him, and let him go*'" (again John 11:44), the implication being that the body was carefully bound to preserve and protect it, although it was not wrapped so tightly that he was unable to walk from the tomb.

36

In the account of our Lord's resurrection it clearly states once again that a separate cloth was used to cover Jesus' face. John 20:6-7 records in great detail that, *'Then Simon Peter came, following him, and went into the tomb. He saw the linen cloths lying there, and the face cloth, which had been on Jesus' head, not lying with the linen cloths but folded up in a place by itself.'*

Nain

In Luke 7:11-17 the Gospel writer records the miracle of the raising of the son of the widow of Nain. In a very graphic way, not only is the miracle an example of Jesus' power in raising the dead and a vindication of his claim to be the Messiah, it is also a vivid illustration of the way that he can spiritually raise sinners to new life.

Normally, touching a bier would ceremonially defile the person involved, but our Lord Jesus had the power over death such that just a few words from him not only banished all defilement, but ultimately death itself.

37

We are told in the account that the body was carried out by bearers and these would generally be members of the close family. In New Testament times biers were seldom used and when one was employed it would frequently be because the body had to be brought a considerable distance. Typically on those occasions when biers were used they would either be open ones or else simply a board upon which the body was laid. It would not be an enclosed coffin in the accepted Western definition of the term. The funeral cortège on this occasion was, we are informed, accompanied by a 'considerable crowd' and this would consist of family, friends, neighbours and any others who wished to pay their last respects to the deceased.

BODIES WHICH HAVE BEEN TOTALLY DESTROYED

Sadly, there are instances when the body of the deceased person is totally destroyed by fire, explosion, is lost at sea or devoured by wild animals; and there are those whose remains are physically destroyed by the wilful act of their enemies. The burning at the stake of many of the early Protestant reformers is a classic example. In such instances any remains which do survive should be gathered together carefully and treated with dignity and respect (as was the case with John the Baptist, already referred to). In those instances where nothing whatsoever remains we have to leave the matter with God and trust him in such circumstances. God who created the world and everything in it is fully capable of recovering every atom of a person, wherever it happens to be, and in whatever chemical form it has adopted.

Had God allowed Shadrach, Meshach and Abednego to be consumed in the fiery furnace as a result of them refusing to worship the golden image set up by King Nebuchadnezzar, or permitted Daniel to be devoured in the lions' den for praying to God contrary to the edict of King Darius, it would have posed no problem whatever for God to resurrect whatever remained of them.

We are told that we shall all, believer and unbeliever alike, be resurrected one day to stand before Jesus who will execute judgement. John 5:28-29 says, '*"Do not marvel at this, for an hour is coming when all who are in the tombs will hear his voice and come out, those who have done good to the resurrection of life, and those who have done evil to the resurrection of judgment."*' The fact that the physical body of some people has been destroyed by fire makes no difference whatever. The reprobate may hope that by destroying their earthly bodies they can avoid standing before the judgement seat, but that is erroneous and foolish thinking.

When King Saul was killed by the Philistines (1 Samuel 31:1-13) his enemies cut off his head and fastened his body to the wall of Beth-shan. It is recorded that Saul's body was subsequently recovered at night by the citizens of Jabesh-gilead who burned Saul's body and then buried the bones. It was considered a mark of disrespect not to bury a dead body and on this occasion the burning may have been done in order to hide the mutilation to the disfigured corpse. Verses 11-13 of the passage record: '*But when the inhabitants of Jabesh-gilead heard what the Philistines had done to Saul, all the valiant men arose and went all night and took the body of Saul and the bodies of his sons from the wall of Beth-shan, and they came to Jabesh and burned them there. And they took their bones and buried them under the tamarisk tree in Jabesh and fasted for seven days.'*

In 2 Samuel 2:5 King David commended the people for what they had done, with these words, *'David sent messengers to the men of Jabesh-gilead and said to them, "May you be blessed by the Lord, because you showed this loyalty to Saul your lord and buried him."'* Later on, in 2 Samuel 21:12-14, we read that David took the bones of Saul and of his son Jonathan from the men of Jabesh-gilead and buried them in the tomb of Saul's father, Kish, in Zela in the land of Benjamin.

WHERE OUR MORTAL REMAINS ARE LAID TO REST

In the accounts referred to concerning the kings of Judah, it has been noted that they were buried in the city of David, rather than just anywhere; and it gives the strong indication that the bodies of believers should be gathered together into one place. That is one of the reasons why, over the centuries, graveyards were traditionally established around churches. Cemeteries are also places where the remains of the departed are kept together, and the concept of a place where the dead are set apart and left to lie at peace is a comforting one.

We live in a world of incessant music, noise, bustle and busyness, and graveyards are one of the few remaining places where one can rest awhile in peace and tranquillity and do nothing but sit quietly, reflect, read Scripture and pray. They invariably have benches dedicated to the memory of loved ones for this specific purpose. They are also places where those who have lost relatives come together and on occasion the opportunity may arise to offer a word of comfort to a stranger (2 Corinthians 1:4). Such locations are also a haven for birds and other wildlife which adds to the serenity of the surroundings.

Graveyards and cemeteries are also a visible and tangible reminder that none of us is immortal and that we all need to resolve the matter of our eternal destination before we join those around us.

Cemeteries are places where the living can rest awhile

Although graves are not shrines, they nevertheless do give a focus and a memorial to the life of the individual. There is nothing wrong with visiting the burial place of a loved one to remember them and give thanks to God for their life. Having a focal point where the body of the deceased is known to be resting enables relatives and friends to come to terms with the fact that the person has indeed departed this life. This can be especially helpful when death has taken place in difficult or tragic circumstances.

41

A headstone giving details of the life and death of the departed must surely be a fitting tribute, to all who pass by, of an earthly life created by God. An entry in a Book of Remembrance does not make that same kind of enduring declaration.

In Genesis 35:19-20 we read that Jacob set up a memorial to Rachel: *'So Rachel died, and she was buried on the way to Ephrath (that is, Bethlehem), and Jacob set up a pillar over her tomb. It is the pillar of Rachel's tomb, which is there to this day.'*

BURIAL FOR CRIMINALS AND ENEMIES

The respect that the people of Israel showed for mortal remains was such that it even extended to those who had committed criminal acts that resulted in the death penalty, as the following passage confirms.

In Deuteronomy 21:22-23 God commanded: *"'And if a man has committed a crime punishable by death and he is put to death, and you hang him on a tree, his body shall not remain all night on the tree, but you shall **bury** him the same day, for a hanged man is cursed by God. You shall not defile your land that the Lord your God is giving you for an inheritance'"* (emphasis added).

This is just one of the whole series of laws given in Deuteronomy instructing the Children of Israel on how society should function once they had entered the promised land. From the above passage it is logical to presuppose that if the convicted perpetrators of a capital offence were allowed the ritual of burial after they had paid the ultimate penalty for their crime, then it is logical to assume that the rest of the population were granted the rite of burial as a matter of course.

An awareness of the necessity for all corpses to be buried is affirmed in an event which took place during the reign of King David when he subdued the surrounding nations, including that of Edom (see 2 Samuel 8:14). In 1 Kings 11:14-16 the passage narrates the time when David and his extremely loyal, but exceedingly ruthless, commander Joab fought against Edom (the Edomites were descendants of Esau). It records that Joab and the Israelite army remained in Edom for *six months* until they had slain *every* male there, and verse 15 states: *'For when David was in Edom, and Joab the commander of the army went up to* **bury** *the slain, he struck down every male in Edom'* (emphasis added). As a result of Joab's retribution none of the Edomites were left alive to bury their own dead and consequently Joab and the Israelites buried them. In this particular instance one gets the strongest impression that Joab had more respect for the dead than the living!

The above passages confirm that the Old Testament people of God displayed a reverence for mortal remains which decreed that they must be buried; and that it extended to the worst of criminals and also to their heathen enemies (see also Ezekiel 39:12). In the light of these examples, should not Christians be of a similar mind-set and insist upon burial for their own bodies?

BEREAVEMENT AND MOURNING

Lamenting over the death of a loved one is a natural reaction and it is a cause of great distress to come to the realization that we shall not see that person again in this earthly life. Even if they are a believer, and we know that we shall eventually be reunited with them once again in glory, it is still a testing time. If they do not know the Lord then it only compounds our grief and sorrow all the more.

The Bible gives numerous examples of individuals expressing their grief; for example Abraham when he lost his wife Sarah: *'And Sarah died at Kiriath-arba (that is, Hebron) in the land of Canaan, and Abraham went in to mourn for Sarah and to weep for her'* (Genesis 23:2). To one of the greatest men of faith such as Abraham, the loss of his beloved wife caused him profound sorrow.

Garden of Remembrance

In Genesis 50:11 we read of the mourning over the death and burial of Jacob: *'When the inhabitants of the land, the Canaanites, saw the mourning on the threshing floor of Atad,*

44

they said, "This is a grievous mourning by the Egyptians." Therefore the place was named Abel-mizraim; it is beyond the Jordan.' The footnote informs us that Abel-mizraim means 'mourning (or meadow) of Egypt'.

In 2 Samuel 3:31-32 we read of King David mourning the loss of Abner: *'Then David said to Joab and to all the people who were with him, "Tear your clothes and put on sackcloth and mourn before Abner." And King David followed the bier. They buried Abner at Hebron. And the king lifted up his voice and wept at the grave of Abner, and all the people wept.'*

Our heavenly Father fully understands the grief we bear at such times and one of the comforts that we are promised in eternity is that there shall be no more weeping for, *'"He will wipe away every tear from their eyes, and death shall be no more, neither shall there be mourning, nor crying, nor pain anymore, for the former things have passed away"'* (Revelation 21:4). What consoling words these are to believers at a time of sorrow.

The period of mourning for Jacob was seventy days (Genesis 50:3) followed by a further seven days (Genesis 50:10). For Aaron it was thirty days (Numbers 20:29) and it was also thirty days for Moses (Deuteronomy 34:8). In the case of Saul it was seven days (1 Samuel 31:13), although this shortened period of time may have been as a result of the impending danger the nation was facing at the time. Notice, however, that in all these instances there is a time limit set after which mourning ends. Mourning is not intended to go on for ever.

The Old Testament lists various customs which the Jewish nation followed at a time of bereavement including: wailing and lamenting (Genesis 50:10, see also Acts 8:2), rending the clothes (Genesis 37:34), dressing in sackcloth (Genesis 37:34 again), employing mourners (Ecclesiastes 12:5 and Jeremiah 9:17), dressing in mourning garments (2 Samuel 14:2), fasting (1 Samuel 31:13) and mournful laments (2 Chronicles 35:25; and Jeremiah 9:20); although not every ritual was adhered to at every death.

The raising of Jairus' daughter by Girolamo Muziano (1532-1592)

In the New Testament account of when our Lord raised the ruler's daughter to life it is recorded that the mourning and wailing was to the accompaniment of flutes (Matthew 9:23).

We have to remark that if death caused such deep grief and sorrow for the people of God, we should not be shocked, embarrassed or ashamed if we display a similar reaction. It is the natural way to respond to tragic circumstances and any attempt to suppress those feelings very often results in psychological problems later on.

One of the positive benefits of attending a funeral service and committal is that, by seeing the mortal remains of a loved one carefully put to rest, it enables us to draw a line under the sad event and then move forward.

Chapter 5

BURNING IN THE BIBLE

As we shall shortly see, burning is used in many places in Holy Scripture as a picture of God's displeasure and his judgement on the reprobate, as is also the curse of bodies not being recovered or buried.

THE WRATH OF GOD

The Bible is God's self-disclosed revelation of his character.[4] It tells us that, among other things, he is a Holy God, a God of justice and that he is also a God of love. His holiness is such that he is altogether pure and righteous to a degree that the finite, human mind cannot fathom. Consequently he is unable to countenance sin and wickedness; he is deeply angry with sinners and he abhors their sin (Psalm 7:11); and they will suffer his wrath and anger unless they turn to him in repentance and faith. Those who approach him casually or irreverently can have little comprehension of just how holy God really is (see Isaiah 6:1-5).

God is also a God of absolute justice who rightfully demands that sin is punished. His verdict is always correct, the sentence is always appropriate, there is no appeal to a higher court, and there is never a miscarriage of justice. God cannot simply excuse sin and ignore it; to do so would be contrary to his nature. The penalty that sin rightly deserves has to be paid and that punishment can either be paid by the sinner himself or by a substitute on his behalf.

The good news of the gospel, however, is that God is also a God of love. His love is so vast that he has provided a way of salvation for guilty sinners who could do nothing to redeem themselves. That way was by sending his only Son, Jesus Christ, to live a sinless life and then to die on Calvary's cross in their place.

Once sinners genuinely repent and believe the gospel, their sin is atoned for and Jesus' perfect righteousness is substituted in place of their own unrighteousness. Until that happens, however, God's wrath remains upon them as the Bible clearly states: *"'Whoever believes in the Son has eternal life; whoever does not obey the Son shall not see life, but the wrath of God remains on him'"* (John 3:36). The apostle Paul says the same thing, *'For the wrath of God is revealed from heaven against all ungodliness and unrighteousness of men, who by their unrighteousness suppress the truth'* (Romans 1:18). For a graphic description of God's wrath and vengeance against his enemies, take a moment to read the devastating words of Isaiah 63:1-6. They portray the Lord Jesus returning victorious from the final battle with his clothes spattered with the blood of his foes. It is a stark reminder of the imperative of laying hold of his free gift of grace without delay, and becoming his friend instead of being his enemy, whilst the offer is still available.

God's wrath against the disobedient and their disobedience is often portrayed in Scripture as a *burning* anger. The following passages are typical examples.

In Exodus 32:11 we read: *'But Moses implored the Lord his God and said, "O Lord, why does your wrath burn hot against your people, whom you have brought out of the land of Egypt with great power and with a mighty hand?"'*

Lych Gate at Thornton, Leicestershire

Psalm 78:49, recounting God's anger against Pharaoh and the Egyptians at the time of the ten plagues says this, *'He let loose on them his burning anger, wrath, indignation, and distress, a company of destroying angels.'*

The psalmist Asaph records these words concerning God's anger and judgement in Psalm 74:1: *'O God, why do you cast us off for ever? Why does your anger smoke against the sheep of your pasture?'*

Another psalmist, this time Ethan, said much the same thing in his distress with these imploring words, *'How long, O Lord? Will you hide yourself for ever? How long will your wrath burn like fire?'* (Psalm 89:46).

49

After the exodus, when the Children of Israel were journeying to the promised land, they grumbled and provoked the Lord to anger. In Numbers 11:1 we are told: *'And the people complained in the hearing of the Lord about their misfortunes, and when the Lord heard it, his anger was kindled, and the fire of the Lord burned among them and consumed some outlying parts of the camp.'* On this occasion not only was the Lord's anger kindled, but he also used burning in his judgement against his rebellious people.

BURNING IS OFTEN ASSOCIATED WITH JUDGEMENT

The burning of bodies by fire is associated with God's anger and as a punishment for gross sin throughout Scripture and it is, in effect, a picture of hellfire as opposed to something slowly and gently returning to the earth to decay naturally and peacefully.

The Levitical law states in Leviticus 20:14: *'"If a man takes a woman and her mother also, it is depravity; he and they shall be burned with fire, that there may be no depravity among you."'*

Further on, in Leviticus 21:9, it records: *'"And the daughter of any priest, if she profanes herself by whoring, profanes her father; she shall be burned with fire."'*

In Joshua 7:25, when the Israelites had been defeated at Ai as a result of Achan's sin in keeping some of the plunder after the battle of Jericho, we are told that, when Achan had been discovered as the guilty party, *'And Joshua said, "Why did you bring trouble on us? The Lord brings trouble on you today." And all Israel stoned him with stones. They burned them with fire and stoned them with stones.'*

Gilroes Crematorium, Leicester

At the end of the Old Testament, speaking of the Day of the Lord in Malachi 4:1, the prophet speaks these dreadful words of judgement, with God finally consuming by fire all those who are his enemies: *"'For behold, the day is coming, burning like an oven, when all the arrogant and all evildoers will be stubble. The day that is coming shall set them ablaze, says the Lord of hosts, so that it will leave them neither root nor branch.'"*

These examples of punishment by burning are a vivid illustration of God's intense, but justified, wrath against evil and godless people.

BURNING OF OTHER THINGS BY FIRE

In order to cover the subject comprehensively, we will now look at instances of things other than human bodies being burned by fire.

At the first Passover in Egypt, nothing of the sacrificial lamb was to remain until morning; anything that was left over was to be burned (Exodus 12:10).

The Old Testament Levitical sacrifices entailed the burning of the offering by fire. One of the consequences of the offering being burnt up was that it was totally consumed and nothing would remain of that part which could be put to any other purpose.

On many of the occasions when God commanded the Israelites to get rid of idols, he commanded that they were to be burned with fire. This was a symbol of the abomination that idolatry is to him, his abhorrence of it, and the deceptive and corrupting influence it can be. In Deuteronomy 7:5 God commanded: *"'But thus shall you deal with them: you shall break down their altars and dash in pieces their pillars and chop down their Asherim and burn their carved images with fire.'"* Later on in the same chapter (v. 25) it records: *"'The carved images of their gods you shall burn with fire. You shall not covet the silver or the gold that is on them or take it for yourselves, lest you be ensnared by it, for it is an abomination to the Lord your God.'"*

Again, in Deuteronomy 12:3, it commands: *"'You shall tear down their altars and dash in pieces their pillars and burn their Asherim with fire. You shall chop down the carved images of their gods and destroy their name out of that place.'"*

Finally we are told in 2 Peter 3:7-10 that when Jesus returns at the end of the gospel age to wrap up the events of history, the present heavens and earth will be totally destroyed by *fire* and that they will be replaced by a new heaven and a new earth. Verse 10 of the passage records this: *'But the day of the Lord will come like a thief, and then the* *heavens will pass away with a roar, and the heavenly bodies will be **burned up** and dissolved, and the earth and the works that are done on it will be exposed'* (emphasis added).

TWO EXAMPLES OF GOD DESTROYING BY FIRE

At the beginning of history in Genesis, and again at the end of history in Revelation, we are given two detailed and very graphic accounts of God totally destroying evil by fire.

In Genesis chapters 18 and 19 we learn that as a result of their gross sin and wickedness, God decides to punish and destroy the cities of Sodom and Gomorrah by fire. From that judgement only Lot and his two daughters escape and are saved by the two angels. Even Lot's wife, who could not bear to leave her sin behind and looked back, was turned into a pillar of salt. Genesis 19:27-28 records: '*And Abraham went early in the morning to the place where he had stood before*

Salt Sea with pillars of salt

53

the Lord. And he looked down toward Sodom and Gomorrah and toward all the land of the valley, and he looked and, behold, the smoke of the land went up like the smoke of a furnace.'

In Revelation chapters 19 and 20 we have the prophetic picture of the final events of history with the return of the Lord Jesus Christ in glory to defeat his foes, and the final judgement and the consignment of the devil, his angels and all unregenerate people to the lake of fire. Only those believers who have been purchased by the blood of Christ are saved from this ultimate destruction. Revelation 20:15 testifies: *'And if anyone's name was not found written in the book of life, he was thrown into the lake of fire.'*

These two passages need to be read in their entirety to grasp the dreadful picture of destruction which they portray.

Cremation chimney

In the light of these episodes the question has to be asked: if God uses fire as judgement in this way, should Christians voluntarily submit their mortal remains to the same sort of treatment?

It may not be a well-known fact, but after bodies have been cremated some of the larger bones will still remain intact, and these are subsequently ground down in a machine called a cremulator, essentially a high-speed blender, to give the fine powder which we traditionally associate with 'ashes'. One must seriously question whether this act shows the corpse any respect whatsoever.[5]

GOD'S CONDEMNATION OF BURNING A BODY

In the Old Testament we read that God sent the prophet Amos to the northern kingdom to pronounce judgement on Israel, Judah and the surrounding nations. Included in this judgement was that of their near neighbour, the nation of Moab.

The primary reason singled out for punishing Moab was because they had burned the remains of the king of Edom as the following passage informs us: *'Thus says the Lord: "For three transgressions of Moab, and for four, I will not revoke the punishment, because he burned to lime the bones of the king of Edom"'* (Amos 2:1). The hatred that Moab had against Edom was vengeful to the point that even death did not put an end to it; they had to exact further retribution on the lifeless body of the king. As a result God responded in judgement: *"'So I will send a fire upon Moab, and it shall devour the strongholds of Kerioth, and Moab shall die amid uproar, amid shouting and the sound of the trumpet; I will cut off the ruler from its midst, and will kill all its princes with him," says the Lord'* (Amos 2:2-3). Scripture is silent elsewhere about this event although there may be a connection with the following episode.

In 2 Kings 3:1-27 it records the account of when Mesha, king of Moab, went out to face the combined armies of Israel, Judah and Edom. During this campaign Mesha made a burnt offering of his own son to Chemosh (the Moabite god) after

The Moabite Stone

he saw that the battle was going against him: *'When the king of Moab saw that the battle was going against him, he took with him 700 swordsmen to break through, opposite the king of Edom, but they could not. Then he took his oldest son who was to reign in his place and offered him for a burnt offering on the wall'* (vv. 26-27).

The burning of the bones of the Edomite king as a sacrifice to Chemosh, and the sacrificial offering by King Mesha of his own son (which ultimately prompted the withdrawal of the opposing forces), both incurred God's wrath such that we are clearly told by Amos that the act of burning bodies, especially in such a pitiless fashion, brings the severest retaliation from God.

The latter event is recorded on one of the oldest stone tablets to be discovered in the Middle east, the Moabite Stone, which was unearthed at the ancient site of Dibon,

Jordan in 1868. The artefact has been dated at around 840 BC and it details several of the events of King Mesha's reign.[6] What is significant of the find is that it contains what is as yet the earliest, and undisputable, extra-biblical reference to Yahweh. A portion of the English translation of the text by Rev. James King in 1878 reads as follows, *'And Chemosh said to me, Go take Nebo against Israel, and I went in the night and I fought against it from the break of day till noon, and I took it: and I killed in all seven thousand men...women and maidens, for I devoted them to Ashtar-Chemosh; and I took from it the vessels of Jehovah, and offered them before Chemosh.'*

DEFILEMENT BY CREMATION

When King Josiah came to the throne of Judah it was at a time when the nation was in the grip of apostasy, and idol worship was rampant. After the Book of the Law had been found in the temple and read to Josiah, the king humbled himself and made this covenant: *'...to walk after the Lord and to keep his commandments and his testimonies and his statutes with all his heart and all his soul, to perform the words of this covenant that were written in this book'* (2 Kings 23:3).

Josiah purged the land of idolatry as part of the wide-ranging reforms that he introduced; by removing the high places, cutting down the Asherim and the carved and metal images, and chopping up the altars of Baal and the incense altars (2 Chronicles 34:1-7). Knowing how easily the people had slipped back into idolatry on previous occasions, Josiah desecrated the places of idol worship. At Bethel he pulled down the altar and burned it, reducing it to dust, and after he had done that he removed the bones of the wicked priests of

Bethel from their tombs and had them burned on the idolatrous altar there in order to defile it. The burning of human bones on the altar was a specific means of despoiling it (see 2 Kings 23:15-16).

NON-BURIAL CONSIDERED A CURSE

In several places in Scripture the concept of the mortal body not being buried was considered to be a curse. The examples given here are typical.

In Deuteronomy, after giving the blessings for obedience to the law, it also records the curses for disobedience, one of them being, *"And your dead body shall be food for all birds of the air and for the beasts of the earth, and there shall be no one to frighten them away"* (Deuteronomy 28:26).

King Solomon has these disturbing words to say about those who appear to have the best in life but are spiritually bankrupt and end up having no burial: *'If a man fathers a hundred children and lives many years, so that the days of his years are many, but his soul is not satisfied with life's good things, and he also has no burial, I say that a stillborn child is better off than he'* (Ecclesiastes 6:3). Solomon considered that to die without a respectful burial was worse than being born dead!

At the end of the reign of King Ahab, one of the sons of the prophets was instructed, by Elisha, to pronounce this curse upon Queen Jezebel, probably the most wicked queen of all, for the evil she had done and to avenge the blood of the prophets and servants of the Lord: *'"And the dogs shall eat Jezebel in the territory of Jezreel, and none shall bury her"'* (2 Kings 9:10).

That curse came to pass when she was thrown down from her window by the eunuchs and dogs did indeed eat her. When they went out to bury her, all that was left was her skull, feet and the palms of her hands. 2 Kings 9:37 pronounces her end thus: *"and the corpse of Jezebel shall be as dung on the face of the field in the territory of Jezreel, so that no one can say, This is Jezebel."'*

Jezreel

Jeremiah prophetically records the double curse of a) not being gathered and b) not being buried but simply left on the ground as refuse, when he describes the fate of the enemies of the Lord: *"'And those pierced by the Lord on that day shall extend from one end of the earth to the other. They shall not be lamented, or gathered, or buried; they shall be dung on the surface of the ground"'* (Jeremiah 25:33).

After the last great battle, recorded in the book of Revelation, when God's enemies are defeated when our Lord Jesus finally returns as the King of kings and Lord of lords, we are informed: *'And the rest were slain by the sword that came from the mouth of him who was sitting on the horse, and all the birds were gorged with their flesh'* (Revelation 19:21). One aspect of their judgement and punishment was that they were not to be buried.

From these passages one certainly gains the strongest impression that for bodies not to be 'gathered' or buried is indeed a curse.

Chapter 6

BIBLICAL TEACHING ABOUT ETERNAL MATTERS

The whole message of the Bible, from beginning to end, is bound up with our standing before God and its teaching about the absolute necessity of repentance for our sin and faith in Jesus Christ as Saviour in order to avoid a lost eternity in hell. Much of this teaching uses the image of burning; either as a reality or as a metaphor.

NEW TESTAMENT TEACHING ABOUT THE UNREGENERATE

John the Baptist, as the forerunner of the Messiah, gave this solemn picture of Christ and his judgement on the reprobate in Luke 3:17 when he announced that Jesus would '"*...gather the wheat into his barn, but the chaff he will burn with unquenchable fire*"'.

Much of the time that Jesus spent teaching the crowds who surrounded him was to urge them to have faith in him as their Saviour. That was in order that the penalty for their sins could be atoned for as a result of his sacrificial death on the cross, and so that his perfect righteousness could be imputed to them. He was constantly warning the people to avoid punishment in hell with its eternal fires (see for example Mark 9:42-50).

In the account that Jesus told of the rich man and Lazarus, in Luke 16:19-31, although we are not told specifically whether the beggar Lazarus was buried, we *are* told that the rich man was buried. Jesus told his hearers that the selfish and unrepentant rich man who ended up in the torment of hell was, *"...in anguish in this flame"* (v. 24).

Olive trees in the Garden of Gethsemane where Jesus spent his last hours

In the parable of the wheat and tares Jesus gave this vivid illustration of what will happen to the unregenerate, again using fire as an illustration: *"...at harvest time I will tell the reapers, Gather the weeds first and bind them in bundles to be burned, but gather the wheat into my barn"* (Matthew 13:30).

In John 15:6 Jesus said this of people who are not in Christ: *"If anyone does not abide in me he is thrown away like a branch and withers; and the branches are gathered, thrown into the fire, and burned."*

Hebrews 6:8 uses the same illustration when it talks about those who have heard the message of the gospel, appear to have accepted it, but in the end reject it: *'...But if it bears thorns and thistles, it is worthless and near to being cursed, and its end is to be burned.'*

As a result of Jesus' teaching, the disciples would have been very familiar with the concept of fire being used in judgement. Towards the end of our Lord's ministry, when he had set his face to go to Jerusalem, and the Samaritan village rejected the messengers who Jesus had sent before him to make preparations, James and John wanted to curse the village by *fire*. Luke 9:54 records: *'And when his disciples James and John saw it, they said, "Lord, do you want us to tell fire to come down from heaven and consume them?"'*

JESUS'S WORDS TO THOSE WHO WOULD FOLLOW HIM

During New Testament times the ritual of burial not only had spiritual connotations; the pattern had become so deeply ingrained into contemporary Jewish culture that it is difficult to visualize a situation where cremation would even have been contemplated. This was demonstrated during the warnings that Jesus gave to the crowds of the cost of following him where burial is presupposed.

We read that after Jesus had set out to go to Jerusalem he called several of those who followed him to be his disciples, all of whom gave different excuses. Scripture records Jesus' words to one man: *'To another he said, "Follow me." But he said, "Lord, let me first go and **bury** my father." And Jesus said to him, "Leave the dead to **bury** their own dead. But as for you, go and proclaim the kingdom of God"'* (Luke 9:59-60, emphases added). It was quite possible that the man's father was not yet dead but rather he was waiting to receive his inheritance before following Christ.

As a result of hearing Jesus' teaching and seeing his miracles, just as today, many who professed that they would forsake all and follow him were in reality unwilling to submit to the commitment that this would entail. Jesus said these challenging words about becoming his disciple: *"Whoever does not bear his own cross and come after me cannot be my disciple. For which of you, desiring to build a tower, does not first sit down and count the cost, whether he has enough to complete it?"'* (Luke 14:27-28).

To this day most devout Jews continue to observe the custom of burial and many who live in the land of Israel take steps to ensure that they are buried on the Mount of Olives,

Jewish graves on the Mount of Olives

outside the walls of the old city of Jerusalem. The reason for choosing this site is that they believe, from the prophecy of Zechariah 14:1-4, that this is the location where their long-awaited Messiah will in due time enter the world.

A PASSAGE FROM 1 CORINTHIANS

There is a passage in the New Testament epistles in which the apostle Paul makes reference to his body being burned which, for the sake of comprehensiveness, needs to be considered. It is important to observe at the outset that the primary theme of this passage is the subject of love, rather than the disposal of mortal remains.

In 1 Corinthians 13:3 the apostle says these words: *'If I give away all I have, and if I deliver up my body to be burned, but have not love, I gain nothing.'* Here Paul is not saying that there is any merit in favour of bodies being burned, but rather he is emphasizing the point that love is the goal that Christians should strive to attain. He considered that even if he should suffer and be martyred for the faith by burning (as happened at the time to many Christians at the hands of the Romans), without love there is no virtue.

From the context of the passage, we can surely surmise that Paul is *not* giving any instruction that he wants his body to be burned or that he is commending cremation in any way.

BURIAL AS AN ILLUSTRATION OF THE RESURRECTION

Our Lord used the picture of burial as an illustration of the resurrection in his teaching about his own death. He described in John 12:20-26 how that, in the same manner that a seed of grain is planted and dies and subsequently brings forth a rich harvest, so also his sacrificial death would result in the salvation of many. Verse 24 of the passage says, *"'Truly, truly, I say to you, unless a grain of wheat falls into the earth and dies, it remains alone; but if it dies, it bears much fruit.'"*

The empty tomb: detail from stained glass window at Gaulby, Leicestershire

Similarly in his first letter to the Corinthians, the apostle Paul likens our mortal bodies to a seed of wheat or some other grain which is sown into the earth and which afterwards corrupts and dies; but from it the new stalk of grain emerges and grows into the full plant which produces a harvest. The apostle points out that, in exactly the same way, the natural bodies of believers are sown into the earth and corrupt and perish; but from those perishable remains the new imperishable spiritual body will emerge and burst forth in glory (see 1 Corinthians 15:35-49).

BAPTISM, BURIAL AND RESURRECTION

At this point it is perhaps relevant to note the parallels that exist between baptism and burial and resurrection.

The River Jordan at Yardenit: the suggested site of Jesus' baptism

In Romans 6:4 the apostle Paul says these words, *'We were buried therefore with him by baptism into death, in order that, just as Christ was raised from the dead by the glory of the Father, we too might walk in newness of life.'* The rite of baptism by immersion is a beautiful picture (at least to western eyes) of the believer who has died to sin (buried in the waters of baptism) and is subsequently raised from death into a new life of righteousness in Jesus Christ

67

(emerges a new creation from the waters). Paul repeats the same imagery in Colossians 2:12 when he states: *'...having been buried with him in baptism, in which you were also raised with him through faith in the powerful working of God, who raised him from the dead'.*

It is necessary to point out that the focus of the foregoing passage concerns the absolute certainty of the resurrection rather than giving instructions about the actual *method* of baptism.[7] Although baptism presents a vivid picture to western believers where bodies of the deceased are buried beneath the ground, it is one that would be alien to Paul's first readers where laying corpses to rest in caves and sepulchres was the recognized practice.

When the saints of old were buried it was for sound reasons, they were not simply following established tribal custom; they were asserting their belief in the sure and certain hope of the resurrection to come.

At that time our mortal bodies will be 'changed' — not exchanged — in the twinkling of an eye into imperishable, immortal bodies. The time it will take for this to happen is not just the fraction of a second that it takes to blink, but the fraction of a millisecond it takes for a beam of light to glance off the pupil of an eye! Paul describes it like this in 1 Corinthians 15:51-53: *'Behold! I tell you a mystery. We shall not all sleep, but we shall all be changed, in a moment, in the twinkling of an eye, at the last trumpet. For the trumpet will sound, and the dead will be raised imperishable, and we shall be **changed**. For this perishable body must put on the imperishable, and this mortal body must put on immortality'* (emphasis added). The power involved to do this must be immense, but to the God who created the entire universe in six days by the word of his mouth all things are possible.

The saints of old saw this resurrection by faith: Job, when he declared that he would see his Redeemer after his flesh had been consumed; Joseph, when he gave his instructions about his bones; and David, in Psalm 16:10, with the prophetic, Messianic words: *'For you will not abandon my*

Burial affirms the believer's confidence in the Resurrection

soul to Sheol, or let your holy one see corruption.' As believers today, we too declare our faith when we insist that we are buried in the absolute certainty of the future resurrection. The whole imagery is lost with the cremation process — how can the process of cremation be equated with the body dying, being buried and then subsequently being resurrected into new life?

PICTURES OF THE SECOND ADVENT

We are told in Matthew 27:52-53 that at the precise moment of Christ's death on the cross, the curtain of the temple was torn in two, from top to bottom, the earth shook and the rocks were split. Simultaneously many tombs were opened and the bodies of 'many' saints were raised to life and went into the city (Jerusalem) and appeared to 'many' people (one speculates whether godly Simeon and Anna, who would have been long dead by this time, would be among those resurrected saints).

Jerusalem

This incident is recorded only in Matthew's Gospel and we are not told how long these saints had been in their graves, what they did in the city, or subsequently what happened to them. We are not told either if they had natural or resurrection bodies, or whether they were afterwards

70

translated into glory; it is a mystery that we can only wonder at. Nevertheless it must have been a momentous occurrence and the mental picture portrayed here gives us a brief glimpse of what will happen when our Lord Jesus finally returns to earth a second time when *all* of his followers will be instantaneously resurrected with glorious new bodies to meet him in the air (1 Thessalonians 4:15-17). What glory that will bring to our exalted Saviour!

In some way cremation just does not seem to fit into this beautiful and triumphant picture of the climax of redemptive history.

The traditional arrangement of churchyards, with the graves generally facing towards the east, expresses the confidence of believers in our Lord's promise that he will one day return, in the same way that he ascended into heaven, to gather his elect. The thinking was that, by looking in this direction, they will be the first to see him appear as they are resurrected from their tombs (see Matthew 24:27; and Ezekiel 43:1-2). Often church ministers would be buried facing in the opposite direction in order that, at Christ's Second Advent, they will be facing their flock once again to lead them into glory.

THE APOSTLES' CREED

Probably the most well-known and widely believed of all the creeds of the Christian faith is the *Apostles' Creed* which sums up, in a few short sentences, the vital elements of what we believe. Amongst its declarations is the section which refers to our Lord Jesus Christ and the fact that he was buried (emphasis added):

[I believe] ... in Jesus Christ His only Son our Lord, who was conceived by the Holy Ghost, born of the virgin Mary, suffered under Pontius Pilate, was crucified, dead and **buried**. He descended into hell. The third day He rose again from the dead. He ascended into heaven and sitteth on the right hand of God the Father Almighty. From thence He shall come to judge the quick and the dead.

Notice that the godly men who devised this litmus test of genuine belief, rather than simply asserting that Jesus was crucified and was subsequently resurrected to life, felt the necessity of affirming the fact that Jesus was actually buried.

One wonders just how many of those who recite what they believe in the words of this great creed, week by week, make any stipulation about what is to happen to their own mortal body.

Chapter 7

CONTEMPORARY VIEWS ON BURIAL AND CREMATION

In order to make this study as balanced as possible, it is necessary to address some of the views that people hold about burial and cremation nowadays before coming to any final conclusion.

RESPONSES TO PROPOSALS IN FAVOUR OF CREMATION

The most common arguments presented in favour of cremation, as opposed to burial, generally take the following lines. A response to each of the specific proposals is offered below:

• *Cremation is more hygienic.* It is granted that all germs and bacteria will probably be destroyed by placing the body in an incinerator; but natural decomposition, over time, will do pretty much the same thing. Burial grounds are inherently no more (or less) unhygienic than anywhere else.

• *Cremation is only hastening the natural decomposition of the remains to dust that would take place in any case.* That may well be so, but in itself it cannot be any warrant for the practice. In reality, after a cremation, what is left are bone fragments rather than 'dust'.

• *Cremation is cheaper.* In view of the true and eternal worth and significance of a life created by God, and the great cost it took to redeem Christians, saving a few pounds seems to be a somewhat worldly and spurious justification.

• *Cremation saves the space taken up by burial plots.* In reality, churchyards and cemeteries take up comparatively little room compared with other open spaces. As an aside, they are often a haven for the living to rest awhile in peace and apart from the general busyness of life. In many instances a burial plot is used to bury the ashes after a cremation which negates this proposition!

Cemetery area set apart for the burial of ashes

• *Cremation is the 'modern' option.* It is a fact that the first cremation in the United States took place in 1876 and in England cremation only became legal as late as 1884, and so cremation is indeed a 'modern' phenomenon.[8] The question that needs to be posed, however, is not whether cremation is modern, but whether it is right!

• There is the argument that, because decaying corpses are not a pretty sight, *by incinerating the remains it eliminates any unpleasant visual aspect of the deceased*. To counter that notion we have to respond by saying that when a person is buried they are left in the ground to decompose naturally. We do not dig up decaying bodies to look at them. In any case, on the very rare occasion when a body has to be exhumed to move it, loved ones do not see it.

Parish Church of St Peter's, Gaulby, Leicestershire, c.1741

• *Most people in the United Kingdom are cremated these days.*[9] That may well be true, but by the same token one could say that today most people in this country are atheists; but that does not necessarily mean that they are right.
• *Cremation is the simplest option.* It is true that cremation does eliminate the necessity of choosing the graveyard or

cemetery, deciding which plot to have, and arranging for the grave to be opened. There is also the choice and wording for the headstone which needs to be decided. Nevertheless these are everyday procedures for a funeral director and it is his duty to guide the family sensitively and sympathetically through the decision-making process.

• You may have heard the thought expressed by some that they are afraid of being certified dead, being interred in the ground, and subsequently reviving; and *cremation eliminates the terror of waking up entombed by ensuring a swift end*. The chances of this happening are infinitesimally remote. In any case, the body will remain in the mortuary for a week or more before the funeral takes place and humans who are *healthy* cannot normally survive for more than three to five days without water.

• For those who cannot cope with bereavement, *cremation makes it much easier to leave the whole matter with the funeral director to make all the necessary decisions*. Surely, when a relative dies it is our solemn duty to lay any personal feelings aside and put as much effort as required into the funeral arrangements.

Dare one also say it, but where it is later suspected that there may have been foul play, it is possible to exhume a buried body and perform an autopsy to get to the bottom of the matter. When a body has been cremated and the ashes scattered, it precludes any possibility whatsoever of this happening — and possibly of justice being done!

To follow on from this, due to the high temperatures involved in cremation all traces of DNA are destroyed and consequently it is not possible to perform genetic testing from the remains.

THE HUMAN CONSCIENCE

Ingrained within the human conscience are values that govern which practices are deemed to be acceptable and those which are not; and this would certainly seem to apply to the burial/cremation debate. It would perhaps be prudent therefore to spend a few moments considering the mental pictures that burial and cremation portray in the human mind. It must be emphasized that the submissions that follow are ethical in tone rather than scriptural.

'Rest in peace'

On the one hand, we have the image of a coffin being gently lowered into a grave, covered with earth, decked with floral tributes and subsequently left to lie undisturbed over the years, and indeed many centuries.

On the other, the picture is of the coffin being drawn through curtains and surrendered to the industrial process of cremation with its furnaces and other machinery. Despite the very best efforts of those within the cremation business it is not a particularly serene or gentle process; and relatively few funeral-goers have much comprehension of what actually happens to the coffin once they have left the chapel.[10] Many, one would surmise, are far too distressed and distraught to think about what occurs to their loved one prior to the ashes being presented. They simply wish to turn the matter over to the funeral director to finish the job as smoothly as possible.

Those final moments of saying 'farewell' to the mortal remains of a deceased relative or friend can linger in the mind for a very long time afterwards and it is sensible to endeavour to make those thoughts as serene as possible.

It is submitted that, if serious thought is given to the matter, burial must surely be the more appealing and morally acceptable practice of the two.

Chapter 8

CONCLUSIONS TO BE DRAWN

The foregoing chapters have looked at some of the examples and teaching concerning burial as they are revealed in the Bible, and they have also considered the reasons why cremation does not appear to have the blessing of God. It is suggested that it is the obligation of every Christian to consider these things carefully and, having done so, decide how they should respond in a way that is glorifying to Christ. As with all decisions in the Christian life, such matters should be considered prayerfully, with Scripture, taken in context, *always* being the final arbiter.

THE RELEVANCE OF GOD'S WORD

Before coming to a final decision on the subject of whether a Christian should be buried or cremated, it is perhaps appropriate to step back for a moment and consider exactly why Scripture should be our guide in this matter; whether it is still relevant in the twenty-first century; and, if we consider it should be our benchmark, what are the demands that it makes. Listed below are some responses to these key questions:

• The Bible is the only handbook for life which claims to be totally infallible and entirely without error (2 Timothy 3:16-17).

• Scripture should be the Christian's guide for every decision in life (Psalm 119:105).

• The commandments of the Bible are still as relevant today as when they were first given (Matthew 5:17-18).

• Examples in the Bible are set down for a purpose and are there to be followed — they are not recorded by chance or merely for academic interest (Luke 10:36-37; John 13:15).

Rural English cemetery

• The freedom which Christians enjoy in Christ does not give them licence to do as they please (Luke 11:28; 1 Peter 2:16).

• Christians should endeavour to please God in every aspect of their lives (1 Thessalonians 4:1).

• Being obedient to God's Word brings us his blessing and it is a proof of our love for him (Deuteronomy 30:16; John 14:15).

80

PROPOSALS IN FAVOUR OF BURIAL

To sum up the findings of our study, listed below are some of the primary submissions in favour of the proposal that Christians should be buried:

• Man was formed from the dust of the ground and will one day return to it.
• We are made in the image of God and that image is to be respected; not only in life, but in death as well.
• The patriarchs took great pains to ensure that they would be buried.
• When God lay to rest the remains of Moses, he buried him.
• The Lord Jesus set us an example to follow by being buried.
• Believers and their bodies are not their own but they belong to Christ.
• Nowhere in the Bible is there any example of a believer willingly being cremated.
• Burial is a vital part of the picture of the resurrection.
• Burial affirms our confidence in the resurrection.
• Graveyards and cemeteries follow the biblical pattern of having the dead gathered together into one place.
• Our earthly bodies are to be *sown* a natural body before they are raised a spiritual body.

It is suggested that this subject needs to be considered long before the spectre of death approaches the horizon. Bereavement is invariably a traumatic time for those left behind and it is never easy to make balanced and rational decisions at times of stress. It is surely better to consider the issue carefully and unhurriedly, and then come to firm decisions at a time when the mind is free from the mental turmoil and anguish which inevitably accompanies bereavement.

HOW TO RESPOND TO CREMATION

The question arises of how we ought to respond when relatives decide to have a loved one or close friend cremated. It might be that they do have firm views in favour of cremation; or they may have no real interest in the matter one way or the other; or it could possibly be that they take the mercenary view that spending as little as possible on the funeral will increase the size of the resulting inheritance!

If the deceased has specified cremation then we have no option in the matter; but in cases where no stipulation has been made I think it is important that we attempt to reason the facts sympathetically. In order that we are able to do so, it is necessary to study the Scriptures carefully to see what they say, have a clear grasp of the issues (hence this little volume), commit the matter to the Lord in prayer, and endeavour to explain gently, but firmly and biblically, exactly what we believe and why. One never knows, but it could result in an opportunity to explain, at a very poignant time, the hope that we have within us (1 Peter 3:15). We may succeed or we may fail, but nevertheless we should endeavour to explain the issues as best we can.

ONE FINAL AND IMPORTANT QUESTION

It is impossible to leave the crucially important subject of life and death without asking the reader to consider, and be quite certain, that they are truly part of God's family and bound for heaven and, if they are unsure, to seek the Saviour and come to Jesus Christ in repentance and faith *now, 'Seek the Lord while he may be found; call upon him while he is near;'* (Isaiah 55:6)!

The words of Daniel 12:2 have these very challenging words about the final judgement which we all need to consider seriously: *'"And many of those who sleep in the dust of the earth shall awake, some to everlasting life, and some to shame and everlasting contempt."'* There will come a time when we shall all have to stand before God to give an account of our lives.

There is no better place to be at life's end than under the loving protection of Jesus as our Lord and Redeemer. If we

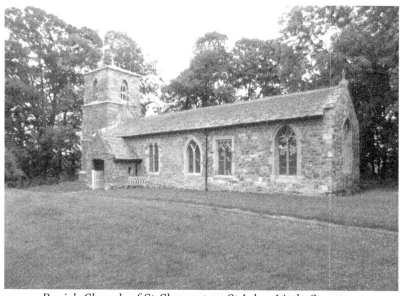

Parish Church of St Clement or St John, Little Stretton, Leicestershire, c.1180

are in Christ we can confidently and triumphantly say together with the apostle Paul:

> *"'O death, where is your victory?*
> *O death, where is your sting?'"*
>
> (1 Corinthians 15:55)

May God lead and guide you as you take the time and effort to consider, diligently and prayerfully, what God's Word has to say on this important subject.

NOTES

Chapter 1

1. The checklist for such a document, which should be signed, dated and sealed, would probably comprise the following:

☐ Where the original copy of the will is lodged.

☐ Instructions to be buried, and *not* cremated.

☐ Details of any funeral plan.

☐ Details of where to be buried (with the plot number if one has been pre-purchased).

☐ The church where the funeral service is to be held, with the preferred minister.

☐ Bible readings and hymns for the service.

☐ Record of significant events, dates and places for the eulogy.

☐ A list of the names and addresses of people to be contacted.

Those who are entrusted with the funeral arrangements will bless you for such forethought.

Chapter 3

2. King James Version: *'about an hundred pound weight'.*

Chapter 4

3. King James Version: *'a pound of ointment of spikenard'.*

Chapter 5

4. *The Attributes of God* by Arthur W Pink (Baker Book House, 1975) is a helpful exposition of the characteristics of God.

5. The actual process of cremation involves placing the coffin in a chamber lined with heat-resistant refractory bricks which is normally fired by oil, gas or propane. The body is incinerated at temperatures of around 1,000°C for approximately 1½ to 2 hours. During this process the soft tissue and internal organs will be vaporized and oxidized, and subsequently discharged with the exhaust gases through the flue system into the atmosphere. After that time there will remain around 4 to 6 pounds (1.8 to 2.7 kg) of bone fragments which are subsequently ground to a fine powder after any metal 'gleanings' have been removed. A tiny residue will be left in the cremation chamber which could possibly be mixed with subsequent cremations. Implanted devices such as pacemakers, spinal cord stimulators and drug reservoirs (all of which could possibly explode) must be removed by the undertaker prior to delivery of the body to the crematorium.

6. The Moabite Stone (or Mesha Stele), dated c.840 BC, was discovered in 1868 and is one of the most significant archaeological artefacts ever discovered inasmuch as it confirms to the world at large what Christians already know — that the Bible is totally inspired in its entirety and can therefore be totally relied upon in the accuracy of its historical accounts as well as in theological matters.

The stone measures 125 cm high and 69 cm wide and is written in a dialect of the Moabite language. There are 34 lines of writing which are legible. When found it was almost intact but it later suffered damage and was broken into several pieces but subsequently reconstructed using a papier mâché 'squeeze' taken before it was smashed. It is universally considered to be genuine. The original has been housed in the Louvre Museum in Paris since 1873.

The translation of the third paragraph by Rev. James King (there are other more modern translations but the readings are all similar) reads as follows (see especially the end of the final sentence):

'And the men of Gad dwelled in the country of Ataroth from ancient times, and the king of Israel fortified Ataroth. I assaulted the wall and captured it, and killed all the warriors of the city for the well-pleasing of Chemosh and Moab, and I removed from it all the spoil, and offered it before Chemosh in Kirjath; and I placed therein the men of Siran, and the men of Mochrath. And Chemosh said to me, Go take Nebo against Israel, and I went in the night and I fought against it from the break of day till noon, and I took it: and I killed in all seven thousand men...women and maidens, for I devoted them to Ashtar-Chemosh; and I took from it the vessels of Jehovah, and offered them before Chemosh.'

Chapter 6

7. For more information see *The Biblical Method of Christian Baptism* by the author (Welford Court Press, 2023).

Chapter 7

8. Statistics published by The Cremation Society of Great Britain listing the percentage of cremations worldwide make thought-provoking reading. The figures for 2011 (when the first edition of this book was published) are shown alongside those for 2021 (or the latest available). They demonstrate clearly that cremation numbers have increased in virtually every country worldwide, in some cases quite dramatically.

Cremation Statistics		
Country	2011	2021
Romania	<1%	<1% ‡
United Arab Emirates	<1%	1% ‡
Trinidad & Tobago	10%	10% ‡
Eire	12%	27%
Italy	14%	33% ‡
France	32%	40% ‡
Norway	37%	46%
United States of America	42%	58%
Russia	48%	29%
Belgium	49% †	66%
China	49%	50% ‡
Netherlands	58%	67%
Canada	59% †	75%
New Zealand	72% †	75% ‡
United Kingdom	74% †	78%
Sweden	79%	84%
Czech Republic	80%	85%
Singapore	80%	83%
Taiwan	91%	97% ‡
Japan	>99%	>99%‡
Figures for 2011 marked † were provisional and those for 2021 marked ‡ are the latest available. The figures have been rounded to the nearest percentage point.		

9. Although hard facts are difficult to obtain, it would appear that people from rural areas (where churches are central to the community) are more likely to be buried than those in urban areas (where churches are less prominent).

Correspondingly, those who consider the subject of death beforehand are more likely to favour burial than those who do not.

10. CAUTION: Pictures and video clips showing the cremation procedure are available to view via the internet, although it should be cautioned that those of a sensitive disposition may find them quite distressing. The reader is therefore respectfully urged to consider the matter very carefully *before* beginning to search for something that is disturbing and could well become impressed upon the memory. For that reason, illustrations of the cremation process have not been reproduced in this volume.

ORDER OF SERVICE FOR A CHRISTIAN FUNERAL

To assist planning the service, listed below is a suggested Order of Service for a simple Christian funeral:

ORDER OF SERVICE

The Sentences

Welcome and Introduction

Hymn: 1

Bible reading: 1

Appreciation/Eulogy

Hymn: 2

Bible reading: 2

Address

Hymn: 3

The Lord's Prayer

Closing prayers

The Blessing

HYMNS FOR FUNERAL SERVICES

The Christian faith has countless beautiful hymns which are very appropriate for funeral services and a few suggestions are listed below:

Abide with me; fast falls the eventide
Henry Lyte (1793-1847)

Amazing grace! How sweet the sound
John Newton (1725-1807)

Be Thou my vision, O Lord of my heart
Ancient Irish, tr. Mary Elizabeth Byrne (1880-1931)

Beneath the cross of Jesus
Elizabeth Cecilia Clephane (1830-1869)

Dear Lord and Father of mankind
John Greenleaf Whittier (1807-1892)

For all the saints who from their labours rest
William Walsham How (1823-1897)

Great is Thy faithfulness
Thomas Obediah Chisholm (1866-1960)

Guide me, O Thou Great Jehovah
William Williams (1717-1791)

How sweet the Name of Jesus sounds
John Newton (1725-1807)

I stand amazed in the presence of Jesus the Nazarene
Charles Hutchinson Gabriel (1856-1932)

Immortal honours rest on Jesus' head
William Gadsby (1773-1844)

Immortal, invisible, God only wise
Walter Chalmers Smith (1824-1908)

In heavenly love abiding
Anna Laetitia Waring (1820-1910)

Lead us, Heavenly Father, lead us
James Edmeston (1791-1867)

Love Divine, all loves excelling
Charles Wesley (1707-1788)

O love that wilt not let me go
George Matheson (1842-1906)

On a hill far away stood an old rugged cross
Rev. George Bennard (1873-1958)

Praise, my soul, the King of Heaven

Henry Lyte (1793-1847)

The day Thou gavest, Lord, is ended

John Ellerton (1826-1893)

The King of love my Shepherd is

Henry Williams Baker (1821-1877)

The Lord's my Shepherd, I'll not want

Francis Rous (1579-1659) revised Scottish Psalter c.1650

Thine be the glory, risen, conquering Son

Edmond Budry (1854-1932), tr. Richard Birch Hoyle
(1875-1939)

To God be the glory

Frances van Alstyne (1820-1915)

When I survey the wondrous cross

Isaac Watts (1674-1748)

BIBLE READINGS FOR FUNERAL SERVICES

Job 19:23-27: "'*Oh that my words were written! Oh that they were inscribed in a book!*'"

Psalm 6:1-10: '*O Lord, rebuke me not in your anger, nor discipline me in your wrath.*'

Psalm 23:1-6: '*The Lord is my shepherd; I shall not want.*'

Psalm 27:1-14: '*The Lord is my light and my salvation; whom shall I fear? The Lord is the stronghold of my life; of whom shall I be afraid?*'

Psalm 34:1-10: '*I will bless the Lord at all times; his praise shall continually be in my mouth.*'

Psalm 42:1-11: '*As a deer pants for flowing streams, so pants my soul for you, O God.*'

Psalm 46:1-11: '*God is our refuge and strength, a very present help in trouble.*'

Psalm 103:8-17: '*The Lord is merciful and gracious, slow to anger and abounding in steadfast love.*'

Psalm 121:1-8: *'I lift up my eyes to the hills. From where does my help come?'*

Psalm 130:1-8: *'Out of the depths I cry to you, O Lord!'*

Psalm 139:1-24: *'O Lord, you have searched me and known me!'*

Ecclesiastes 3:1-22: *'For everything there is a season, and a time for every matter under heaven.'*

John 6:35-40: *'Jesus said to them, "I am the bread of life; whoever comes to me shall not hunger, and whoever believes in me shall never thirst."'*

John 11:17-27: *'Now when Jesus came, he found that Lazarus had already been in the tomb four days.'*

John 14:1-6: *'"Let not your hearts be troubled. Believe in God; believe also in me."'*

Romans 8:28-39: *'And we know that for those who love God all things work together for good, for those who are called according to his purpose.'*

1 Corinthians 13:1-13: *'If I speak in the tongues of men and of angels, but have not love, I am a noisy gong or a clanging cymbal.'*

1 Corinthians 15:42-57: '*So is it with the resurrection of the dead. What is sown is perishable; what is raised is imperishable.*'

1 Thessalonians 4:13-18: '*But we do not want you to be uninformed, brothers, about those who are asleep, that you may not grieve as others do who have no hope.*'

Revelation 21:1-7: '*Then I saw a new heaven and a new earth, for the first heaven and the first earth had passed away, and the sea was no more.*'

THE AUTHOR

Adrian Freer was born and still lives in Leicestershire where he is now retired. He was educated at Loughborough Grammar School and Leicester College of Art & Technology (now De Montfort University).

He had a non-church upbringing and was a member of the Methodist Church before conversion.

After many years in the evangelical movement he settled under the ministry of the late Rev. Ashley F B Cheesman, rector of the Parish of Gaulby, Leicestershire, England from 1988 until 2010.

The Gaulby Parish of Anglican churches was one of the Church of England parishes in the county of Leicestershire which upheld the doctrines of the English Reformers, subscribed to the Thirty-Nine Articles of Religion and used the 1662 *Book of Common Prayer* in its services.

After the untimely death of Rev. Cheesman in 2010 the work of the Gaulby Reformed Evangelical Anglican Fellowship continued for a further nine years until it finally closed in 2019.

Adrian Freer is the author of a number of books including *Quiet Time for Christians: A Practical Guide to Daily Bible Reading and Prayer* (Welford Court Press), *A Biblical Defence of the Sport of Angling* (Welford Court Press), *The Book of Benedictions: A Collection of Blessings from the Holy Bible* (Welford Court Press), *The Biblical Method of Christian Baptism* (Welford Court Press) and *The Moabite Stone and the Holy Bible* (Welford Court Press).

Apart from church responsibilities, Adrian's other interests include fly fishing and fly tying, music, foreign travel and writing. He is married with two daughters and four grandchildren.

For further information visit Adrian Freer's website: www.webdatauk.wixsite.com/adrian-freer

St Peter's Church,
Gaulby, Leicestershire

AUTHOR'S DOCTRINAL STATEMENT

Very often when reading religious books it is not always easy to ascertain the doctrinal position of the author at the outset. Although this will generally become clear as progress through the work is made, it would be useful to have this information beforehand.

All too often statements such as 'Bible Believing' and 'Christian' are made by those who clearly do not really believe that God's Word is inerrant and infallible in its entirety, have any real faith, or sometimes even believe in God.

The author suggests that it would be helpful if books contained a statement of the writer's doctrinal stance. That being the case the author has chosen to state his position here, and in the hope that other writers might do the same:

The author would describe himself as Protestant, evangelical in the 'traditional' meaning of the term, a five-point Calvinist†, one who upholds the doctrines of the Reformers, and subscribes to the Thirty-Nine Articles of Religion.

With regard to controversies at the forefront at the present time: he believes (Scripture teaches) a literal six day creation, the doctrine of election, marriage should *only* be between one man and one woman, church leadership and authority should be restricted to men, and he holds an amillennial eschatological position.*

With reference to the 'Israel' debate he understands that the church, comprising both believing Jews and Gentiles, is the fulfilment of the Old Testament nation of Israel (rather than the current geographical/political state of Israel).

† The book *TULIP: The Five Points of Calvinism in the Light of Scripture* written by Duane Edward Spencer (Baker Books, 1979) explains this issue.

* For a helpful exposition of this subject *The Momentous Event* by W J Grier (Banner of Truth Trust, 1945) is well worth studying.

**St Michael & All Angels Church,
Ilston-on-the-Hill, Leicestershire**

INDEX

St John the Baptist Church,
Kings Norton, Leicestershire

Quiet Time for Christians: A Practical Guide to Daily Bible Reading and Prayer

Adrian V W Freer

Setting aside a regular time each day to read God's Word and have a time of prayer is one of the most valuable disciplines for any Christian if they are to have a closer walk with their Saviour.

The aim of this book is twofold: firstly to assist those who already have a quiet time to make it more profitable and productive, and secondly to persuade those who do not as yet have a regular time alone with God to begin that rewarding and lifelong journey now.

Paperback: 158 pages, 54 illustrations, 6 tables and 1 map

Published by: Welford Court Press   ISBN: 978-1-79899530-3-3

The Book of Benedictions: A Collection of Blessings from the Holy Bible

Adrian V W Freer

The purpose of this book is to assist in the selection of a suitable benediction to conclude church services and when taking prayers.

Extempore and written prayers can be fine, but why settle for second best when the Bible, God's inspired and inerrant Word, contains so many passages that are helpful, challenging and encouraging.

It is the author's sincere prayer that this volume will prove to be a helpful 'on-the-desk' sermon preparation tool for those entrusted with the solemn responsibility of preaching God's Word and also a comforting devotional aid for Christians at large.

Paperback: 96 pages, 25 illustrations

Published by: Welford Court Press   ISBN: 978-0-9520304-6-1

Printed in Great Britain
by Amazon

58246340R00059